The Classic Palmer

The Classic
PALMER

Text by John Feinstein
Photographs by Walter Iooss

STEWART, TABORI & CHANG | NEW YORK

There are many different ways to describe

the manner in which an athlete dominates his sport. There are statistics and records and videotapes that can document one's accomplishments. There are paeans written and film tributes produced and awards presented. There are Halls of Fame to be inducted into and lifetime achievement plaques to be received.

Many athletes deserve—and receive—all these honors.

But the list of athletes for whom the rules of an entire sport have been changed is a short one.

When Babe Ruth hit more home runs in an entire season than the rest of the American League, baseball decided it needed a livelier ball to give other hitters a chance to compete with the Babe. When Lew Alcindor played college basketball at UCLA in the 1960s, the dunk was outlawed to give defenders *some* chance to stop the unstoppable center.

And then there is Arnold Daniel Palmer. In 1980, both the United States Golf Association and the PGA Tour believed there was a market for a golf tour for players who were no longer at their peak physically but could still play the game well and appealed

5

to fans. There was just one problem: the player who defined that sort of appeal and charisma had just turned fifty, and USGA rules defined a senior player as someone who was fifty-five or older.

If fans were going to buy tickets for senior golf or watch it on television, if corporations were going to put up sponsorship money, Arnold Palmer had to be out there playing. It was very simple: without Palmer there would be no Senior PGA Tour. If there was any doubt about that, it vanished after the first U.S. Senior Open was played on the East Course at the famed Winged Foot Golf Club in 1980.

"We had crowds into the dozens—maybe," said David Fay, who was executive director of the USGA for twenty-one years but was at that time assistant executive director. "We had good players in the field, and it was a wonderful golf course. But we didn't have Palmer."

Waiting until Palmer turned fifty-five was not an option if there was going to be a Senior Tour. Thus, the USGA declared, in its wisdom, that professionals (not amateurs) were deemed seniors the day they turned fifty.

"A year later we had the Senior Open at Oakland Hills, and Arnie beat Billy Casper and Bob Stone in a Monday play-off," Fay said. "We had great crowds all week, including Monday. It's probably not unfair to say that if the rules change hadn't been made, there might not be a Senior Open today."

Or a Champions Tour—as the PGA Tour has called its Senior Tour since 2002—which Palmer played on until 2007, drawing

U.S. Open, Oakmont Country Club,
Oakmont, PA, June 1973

huge crowds until the day he finally decided, at the age of seventy-eight, that his game was no longer good enough to be put on public display. What he failed to understand was that the fans didn't care at that stage how many birdies he made—or didn't make. They just wanted to see the King, the leader of Arnie's Army, walk down the fairway.

Through the years there have been numerous arguments on the subject of who the greatest golfer of all time might be. It dates to the question of Bobby Jones versus Walter Hagen, or Ben Hogan versus Byron Nelson and Sam Snead, right to today's Jack Nicklaus–versus–Tiger Woods discussion.

But for the last fifty years there has been absolutely no debate about who is the most *important* golfer of all time. It is Arnold Palmer. They changed the rules of the sport for him. Case closed.

OPPOSITE AND FOLLOWING: U.S. Open, Baltusrol Golf Club, Springfield, NJ, June 1967

Palmer was born into the game of golf.

His father, Milford Jerome "Deacon" Palmer, was both the greens-keeper and the head professional at Latrobe Country Club in the hills of western Pennsylvania. The city of Latrobe is forty miles east of Pittsburgh and was founded in the mid-nineteenth century largely as a railroad town. Its population topped out at about ten thousand, although by the time the census was done in 2000 the official number was 7,634. It is listed in many historical guides as the birthplace of Rolling Rock beer and Arnold Palmer.

Most people would agree that the golfer has played a more significant role in the culture of the country and the world than the beer. Arnold was the oldest of Deacon and Doris Palmer's four children—two boys and two girls. He also spent the most time on his father's golf course. For a large chunk of his childhood, Palmer's family lived in a rented two-story house, for which they first paid fifteen dollars a month, near the 6th tee at Latrobe. Arnold was a teenager before he helped his dad build an indoor bathroom for the house.

Arnold was a golf star almost from birth. He played with other

PGA Championship, Laurel Valley
Golf Club, Ligonier, PA, July 1965

club employees whenever he could and spent just about all his free time working on his swing. He never had a picture-perfect swing by any means. In fact, most golf purists would wince at the way he followed through, contorting his body to get maximum thrust through the ball, then twirling the club at the top more in the manner of someone swishing a sword than finishing a golf swing.

The sheer effort in every swing, the violence of it, would become Palmer's calling card. It was part of the reason he was so often referred to as the game's greatest swashbuckler. His swing looked like that of a dueling pirate, and his fearless style on the golf course backed up the image created by his stroke.

Deacon Palmer was his older son's teacher, mentor, and taskmaster. Not that he ever had to get the boy to work at golf—Arnold loved the game too much to ever think of it as work. But it was Deacon who set the standard Arnold wanted so much to live up to, who made him understand that there was more to the game than blasting the ball as far as he could and making every putt possible.

Arnold has often told the story of the day he threw a club in frustration on the back nine during a match. He went on to win, but that wasn't what his father wanted to discuss on the car ride home.

"If I ever see you throw a club like that again, it will be the last time you play," Deacon Palmer said. "Understood?"

Arnold understood. To get angry on the golf course was acceptable; to put your temper on display was not. Perhaps the world of golf today would be a different place if more players had taken car

U.S. Open, Oakmont Country Club, Oakmont, PA, June 1973

FOLLOWING: U.S. Open, Baltusrol Golf Club, Springfield, NJ, June 1967

rides with Deacon Palmer after losing their tempers on the golf course.

Once he knew his club-tossing days were over, Arnold kept getting better and better at golf. He chose Wake Forest College (now Wake Forest University) in North Carolina and quickly became a star in college golf, winning the Southern Conference Championship as a freshman. (This was before the Atlantic Coast Conference was formed in 1953, when seven schools including Wake Forest split from the Southern Conference.) But his life and his golf career took a horrifying turn when his best friend, Buddy Worsham, and another friend, Gene Scheer, were killed in an accident en route home from a weekend dance at Duke. Worsham had asked Palmer to attend the dance with them, but Palmer had already made Friday-night plans to see a movie with another pal, Jim Flick.

After the deaths of his friends, Palmer had to get away from Wake Forest. There were too many memories. He joined the Coast Guard and continued to play golf during his three years in the service. Then he returned to Wake Forest and won the first Atlantic Coast Conference Golf Tournament in 1954. He left school again that spring, his goal being to win the U.S. Amateur Championship, the one important amateur title that had eluded him.

In those days, winning the Amateur was almost as important as winning the Masters Tournament or the U.S. Open Championship. When Bobby Jones won his "grand slam," in 1930, the four titles that made up the slam were the U.S. and British Amateurs,

U.S. Open, Baltusrol Golf Club,
Springfield, NJ, June 1967

the U.S. Open, and the British Open, as opposed to today's grand slam, which consists of the Masters, the U.S. Open, the British Open, and the PGA Championship. There was no Masters until Jones and Clifford Roberts launched that event in 1934, and the PGA wasn't considered that important, since top amateurs like Jones weren't eligible to play.

In fact, when Ben Hogan won the Masters, the U.S. Open, and the British Open in 1953, there was never any thought that he would try to win the PGA, because the tournament overlapped with the British Open. Very few American pros made the overseas trip in those days. When Hogan won at Carnoustie Golf Links that year, it was his first and only appearance in the British Open. It would not be until the 1960s—after Arnold Palmer began appearing on a regular basis—that most American pros began to make the trip to Great Britain each summer.

"It bothers me when people say I won seven majors," Palmer has often said. "Back when I won the Amateur it was just as important as the professional majors and harder to win, because it was grueling and because of the competition. As far as I'm concerned, I won eight majors, not seven."

In 1954, most of those who contended in the U.S. Amateur were lifelong amateurs or occasional young players who were deciding whether to pursue a pro career. Back then, turning pro wasn't a given for a talented young golfer, because there wasn't that much money to be made on tour. In fact, most pros had to work at least part of the year as club pros. Today, almost anyone

U.S. Open, Olympic Club, San
Francisco, CA, June 1966

who makes it through the first two rounds of stroke play at the Amateur to be one of the sixty-four who move on to match play aspires to play on the PGA Tour.

Palmer's opponent in the thirty-six-hole championship match was a very talented lifelong amateur named Robert Sweeny. A past British Amateur champion, Sweeny was forty-three and an investment banker by trade. He birdied three of the first four holes for a quick three-up lead and looked ready to turn the match into a rout.

Palmer's calling card in his prime would be his ability to come from behind. Perhaps that day at the Country Club of Detroit was the first time he put that ability on display with a lot of people watching. He rallied to take the lead late in the match and won the amateur title on the 36th hole. At the end of that year, he turned pro and began one of the great professional careers in golf history.

It can be argued that Palmer's career has actually been under-rated. How is that possible? Palmer did so much for the game and heightened its popularity so greatly that people often focus on that, rather than what he accomplished on the golf course.

There is no doubting that Palmer's presence changed the PGA Tour forever. Even though the game had plenty of megastars prior to his arrival—Bobby Jones, Walter Hagen, Gene Sarazen, Ben Hogan, Byron Nelson, and Sam Snead among them—none had the charisma and charm that Palmer brought to the table, although if Sarazen's peak years had come during the television era, he might have been almost as beloved a figure as Palmer became.

U.S. Open, Olympic Club, San
Francisco, CA, June 1966

But he wasn't. Palmer arrived on tour just as television cameras appeared in the golf world. The first tournament aired on television was in 1953, when a promoter named George S. May paid ABC thirty-two thousand dollars to broadcast his Tam O'Shanter World Championship—with a then-unheard-of first prize of twenty-five thousand dollars. NBC televised the U.S. Open nationally for the first time in 1954—the same year Palmer won the Amateur. CBS televised the Masters for the first time in 1956. To say that Palmer's emergence as a star was a key to the growth of golf as a TV sport, and in general, is a little like saying the heat of the sun is vital to life on Earth.

That Palmer was the straw that stirred the drink—years and years before Reggie Jackson made the term popular when he came to New York to play baseball—has been agreed on for more than fifty years. If a marketing company had been hired to create the perfect golfer to lead the sport into TV nirvana, they would have created Palmer.

He had the matinee-idol looks that made women swoon and the belt-hitching swagger that made men want to be like him. Women wanted to have a quiet glass of wine with him; men wanted to have a beer with him. He had the look of a guy who grew up in a house without indoor plumbing, of a kid who came from the other side of the tracks but was completely comfortable on your side too. He was a blue-collar guy in a white-collar world.

There was no quit in him. If he fell behind, it just meant his comeback would be that much more thrilling. He wasn't smooth:

PREVIOUS: U.S. Open, Olympic Club, San Francisco, CA, June 1966

U.S. Open, Congressional Country Club, Bethesda, MD, June 1964

he had the arms of a blacksmith and the golf swing of one too. He *didn't* make it look easy, and that made people want to see him win even more.

Beyond that, though, he had an almost unique ability to connect with everyone. Tiger Woods has many of Palmer's qualities—the good looks, the electrifying ability to rally, the willingness to try any shot—but he doesn't connect with people the way Palmer did. In truth, he never wanted to: Palmer looked everyone in the eye and smiled; Woods looks almost no one in the eye. Palmer seemed willing to let everyone into his life; Woods doesn't want anyone near his.

Right from the beginning, Palmer *got* celebrity—he understood it and embraced it.

When Curtis Strange—who always bridled at being a public figure—became the No. 1 player in the world in the 1980s, he complained to Palmer, who had been close to Strange's father, about the responsibilities that came with stardom: signing autographs, dealing with the media, spending time with sponsors. Palmer shrugged and said, "You don't have to do any of that if you don't want to."

Strange was stunned. "I don't?" he said. "How do I not do any of that?"

"Go home," Palmer answered. "Don't get paid to play golf for a living. Don't take money from sponsors. Don't get paid to wear a shirt or a hat or play with a certain kind of golf club or golf ball. Just give all that back and go home. Then you don't have to do any of that anymore."

U.S. Open, Olympic Club, San
Francisco, CA, June 1966

Strange got the message.

Years later, Palmer had a similar talk with Woods, then a rookie pro, in the champions' locker room at Augusta National Golf Club. "It's not fair," Woods complained over lunch after a pre-Masters practice round in 1997. "I can't be a normal twenty-one-year-old." He resented the obligations of fame, just as Strange had: autographs, media, photo shoots for commercials, glad-handing with sponsors.

"You know, Tiger, you're right," Palmer answered. "You aren't a normal twenty-one-year-old. Normal twenty-one-year-olds don't have fifty million dollars in the bank. If you want to be a normal twenty-one-year-old, that's fine—just give the money back."

Palmer never wanted or needed a "normal" life. He never bridled at signing an autograph or doing an interview or spending time with a sponsor. He loved interacting with fans.

"I've always tried to tell the younger guys that if they want the perks of stardom, they have to accept the responsibilities too," he said, long after he had become a superstar. "Everyone wants to make the money, to be adored and cheered, to be treated special everywhere they go. It's understandable. But you can't just go through life taking. At some point you have to give, and what we're asked to give isn't very hard to give."

When Tom Watson first ascended to the role of No. 1 player in the world, he was always cooperative with the media and generous with the fans at the golf course. He considered that part of the job. But he didn't want any intrusions into his private life. He drew a

U.S. Open, Olympic Club, San Francisco, CA, June 1966

FOLLOWING: PGA Championship, Laurel Valley Golf Club, Ligonier, PA, July 1965

line between the public figure and the private one. Palmer thought that was understandable, but he also believed it was unnecessary.

"As a public figure, you're going to give up some of your private life," he said. "But there are moments, like when your kids all jump into bed with you to watch something on television or you're just sitting around the dinner table, that no one can take away from you—no one. That's why I've never worried about that sort of thing."

Which is why Palmer's appearance on the public stage in the mid-1950s could not have been more perfectly timed. He loved the spotlight, and the spotlight loved him. And while there were those—notably the great Ben Hogan—who wondered if Palmer had the golf swing or the game to become a star, Palmer never doubted himself. That self-confidence, along with his desire to prove Hogan and any other doubters wrong, would propel him to heights previously unimagined for a golfer. They would make him Arnold Palmer—the one for whom rules were changed and drinks were named.

There was a joke told often in golf locker rooms in the 1960s: A man dies and goes to heaven. As he walks through the pearly gates, he looks over and sees the driving range. Someone is pounding one three-hundred-yard drive after another but getting angrier each time he hits the ball, and thrashing his driver in frustration.

The new arrival watches this for a moment and then turns to Saint Peter and says, "Who does that guy think he is, God?"

Saint Peter shakes his head and says, "Actually, that *is* God. He thinks he's Arnold Palmer."

Which is a roundabout way of getting back to the question of Palmer being underrated. So much of what has been said and written about him through the years has focused on his magnetic qualities, the magical charisma that created Arnie's Army, that sometimes people forget just how well he played the game.

Consider for a moment just a few of the numbers: He won sixty-two times on the PGA Tour. Only four players in history— Sam Snead (eighty-four times), Jack Nicklaus (seventy-three times), Tiger Woods (seventy-one times), and Ben Hogan (sixty-four times)—won more often. No current PGA Tour player other than Woods has won as many as forty times: Phil Mickelson is second on the active list, with thirty-nine victories.

Palmer also won seven professional major championships and would tell you he left a number of others on the table. On ten other occasions he finished second or tied for second. Win or lose, Palmer almost always made the outcome dramatic. Everyone who follows golf remembers him birdieing the last two holes at Augusta in 1960 to win the Masters and driving the 1st green at Cherry Hills Country Club later that year en route to a final-round 65 that allowed him to pass fourteen players and win the U.S. Open. But they also remember the double bogey 6 in 1961 at the Masters— after he walked over to the ropes to accept congratulations from a friend, something no other player of his caliber would have considered doing—and they remember too the seven-shot lead that

U.S. Open, Congressional Country Club, Bethesda, MD, June 1964

PREVIOUS: U.S. Open, Olympic Club, San Francisco, CA, June 1966

disappeared on the back nine on Sunday during the 1966 U.S. Open at the Olympic Club.

But that was part of Palmer's magic. He was always charging in one direction or another. He never stood in place, was never content to grind out pars. It wasn't his style, and it wasn't what his fans wanted to see. They wanted him trying the impossible shot even when it wasn't the smartest shot. They didn't come to watch Palmer play strategic golf; they came to watch him play memorable golf. Almost always, one way or another, he gave them what they came to see.

He was successful right away once he turned pro, winning the Canadian Open, then one of the most important events on tour, as a rookie in 1955. He won seven more times over the next three years and had established himself as a rising star on the PGA Tour by the time he got to Augusta in 1958. Like anyone who dreamed of greatness—which Palmer had since boyhood—he wanted to win major titles. Even though he thought of the U.S. Amateur as a major, he hadn't won a professional major yet.

Beyond that, he had been stung when he overheard Hogan, after playing a practice round with him, say to someone, "How the hell did that guy get in the Masters?"

Hogan's search for the perfect golf swing has been well documented. To this day, a few insist that they know Hogan's "secret" to the golf swing. He worked for hours and hours on the range, practicing, honing, always searching "in the dirt" for the key. Hogan's approach to the game was probably best summed up by the story

Carling World Open, Oakland Hills
Country Club, Bloomfield Hills, MI,
August 1964

about his response to the question, What is a perfect round of golf?

"A perfect round of golf is an 18," Hogan answered. "Once, I dreamed that I made seventeen straight holes-in-one and lipped out on 18."

The story is still told as proof of just how hard golf is: even the great Hogan couldn't *dream* a perfect round.

Palmer's dreams were very different from Hogan's. For one thing, he never searched for the perfect swing. If Hogan's swing was pure, Palmer's was pure power. He didn't just swing the club, he unleashed it. Hogan never looked off balance; Palmer fre-

British Open, St. Andrews,
Scotland, July 1978

quently looked as if he was going to topple forward when he finished his swing. Hogan viewed Palmer's swing the way an artist might view the work of a housepainter. What he didn't recognize was that Palmer's swing was a masterpiece too—just a completely different kind.

Palmer had already won eight times on tour going into that Masters Tournament in 1958. When Hogan questioned him, it wasn't as if he had just shown up and had a bad day. Which may explain why Hogan's slight made Palmer so angry.

Palmer has often told the story of that day and how it drove him. Each retelling is a little different. Most accounts have Palmer overhearing Hogan say to Jackie Burke after playing a practice round with Palmer on the Tuesday of the '58 Masters, "How the hell did that guy get in the Masters?" Sitting in his home at the Bay Hill Club and Lodge in Orlando, Florida, on a Sunday morning in 1994, Palmer smiled and said, "He said, with my swing, I better go out and look for a job. I never did get around to doing that."

Instead, he won the Masters in 1958 for his first major title. He did it—naturally—in dramatic fashion, although not with the kind of drama he would have preferred. Trailing Ken Venturi by one shot on Sunday, his tee shot flew the 12th green and half embedded in the wet ground on the embankment that ran behind the tiny green. Palmer consulted with one rules official who told him he wasn't entitled to a drop. Believing the official to be incorrect, Palmer played two balls—one from where his tee shot had landed, the other with the drop he thought he was allowed to take.

He made a double bogey 5 with the first ball, a par 3 with the second. It wasn't until three holes later that Masters Tournament cofounders Bobby Jones and Clifford Roberts informed him they had ruled in his favor and that his score on the 12th hole was a three. By then Palmer had reached the par-5 13th hole in two and had dropped an eighteen-foot putt for an eagle. Venturi collapsed after that, and Palmer hung on to beat Doug Ford and Fred Hawkins—who both missed birdie putts on 18 that would have forced a play-off—by one shot for his first major championship victory.

That victory was the beginning of the Palmer Era in golf. More and more tournaments were being televised, and there was no doubt about the game's most telegenic star. Most professional athletes put up with the media and with the adoration of fans. They know that it is part of their job to talk to people and sign autographs. They deal with it in different ways: Phil Mickelson always tells his longtime caddie, Jim Mackay, that he will need at least ninety minutes at the end of a round before he can meet him on the range, because he knows he has to talk to the media and spend forty-five minutes signing autographs. Somewhere in there he will grab something to eat before going to meet Mackay. He sees it as part of his job, and he does it graciously every single day, as opposed to Woods, who often bridles and complains about doing those things.

Palmer *liked* doing those things. Some of it no doubt came from the way he grew up: as a club pro's son. A club pro is the per-

Bing Crosby National Pro-Am,
Pebble Beach Golf Links, Pebble
Beach, CA, January 1966

son who stands around and listens to every member's story about the eagle almost made, the putt for 79 that didn't go in, the horrible break when the ball buried in a bunker, and how they are *this close* to making a breakthrough with their golf swing.

Not only does the club pro listen, he makes the listener believe he honestly cares and can't wait to get back on the practice tee to help turn that 18 handicap into the 14 handicap it really should be. Palmer frequently points out that Deacon Palmer didn't want him in the club pool at Latrobe with the members' kids; he did most of his swimming with other club employees in the streams around the club. He learned early that every member was important and that each story was worthy of attention.

In a sense, Palmer has always treated others the way his father taught him, as if they were all members at Latrobe. Unlike most superstars, he never set himself apart from other players. Just the opposite: he went out of his way to be one of the guys and, as he got older, to counsel younger players on how to act on and off the golf course.

Rocco Mediate, who grew up in Greensburg, Pennsylvania, a couple of towns over from Latrobe, remembers the first time he was invited by a mutual friend to play at Latrobe with Palmer.

"He didn't even tell me we were going to play with him, because he knew I'd freak out and probably not even show up, I'd be so scared," Mediate remembered with a laugh. "I get there and we're walking to the first tee and I see him standing there. I looked at my buddy and said, 'Oh no, you're not serious. I can't do this.'

He just kept walking. I walked on the first tee with my legs shaking. Arnold came over and shook hands and said hello, and I swear to God I felt as if I'd known him all my life. Just like that. He has that unbelievable quality that can make you feel as if you're best friends in about ten seconds—or less.

"By the time I got on the tee to hit my first shot, I felt like I was out playing with a couple of my buddies. It's never changed, except that now that I know him well, he sometimes gives me a hard time about things."

Through the years, Palmer has lectured Mediate on his weight

49

With Gary Player, Baltusrol Golf
Club, Springfield, NJ, August 1964

and his lifestyle, talked to him about living up to his potential as a player, and let him know when he was proud of him and when he was not. Mediate is about as strong willed as anyone on the golf tour; he's not someone who often takes the advice of others. But when Palmer speaks, he listens.

"I know where he's coming from when he talks to me," he said. "I know he genuinely cares. Plus, I know most of the time, even when he's saying things I don't want to hear, that he's right."

Palmer has always done that with younger players: let them know he cared about them and then told them the truth. As intense as his rivalry with Jack Nicklaus was, he set Nicklaus up to be represented by his friend and business partner Mark McCormack, even after initially insisting that McCormack represent only him as a condition of their early partnership. He did the same for Gary Player, which helped both players but also launched McCormack into starting the International Management Group, which eventually became the most powerful sports management entity in the world.

In 1991, when Palmer made the cut at his own tournament—now known as the Arnold Palmer Invitational—at the age of sixty-one, every player in the locker room was thrilled. Palmer had hosted the tournament at Bay Hill beginning in 1979, and it had quickly become one of the players' favorite stops on tour. That was due in part to the quality of the golf course, which Palmer was always tweaking and improving, but mostly it was the opportunity to spend a week knowing that at any moment Palmer might stroll

U.S. Open, Congressional Country Club, Bethesda, MD, June 1964

FOLLOWING: British Open, St. Andrews, Scotland, July 1978

into the locker room or onto the practice tee or ask if you'd like to go play nine holes in a practice round.

"It was just about Arnie in the end," said Jeff Sluman, the 1988 PGA Championship winner. "I mean, let's be honest, we get spoiled every week every place we go, with cars and tickets and free food and pretty much anything we could possibly ask for. But when you're at Arnie's place and he's there all the time, it feels special. *He* makes you feel special. A lot of times when someone running a tournament says, 'Have you got everything you need?' you know it's a rhetorical question. If your answer is anything but 'Yes,

U.S. Open, Oakmont Country Club,
Oakmont, PA, June 1973

everything's great,' they're going to get a glazed look in their eyes and run for cover. When Arnold asks, you know he really wants to know, because if something isn't just right, he's going to be damn sure it gets fixed right away."

On the night that Palmer made that cut at Bay Hill in 1991, Peter Jacobsen went to a local Winn-Dixie. He wanted to get a giant cake so the players could present it to Palmer in the locker room the next day.

"I need a sheet cake for about two hundred people," Jacobsen told the manager.

U.S. Open, Oak Hill Country Club,
Rochester, NY, June 1968

"For when?" the manager asked him.

"Tomorrow morning," Jacobsen answered.

The manager laughed and told Jacobsen that was completely out of the question. "Look, I'm playing at Bay Hill," Jacobsen explained. "Arnie made the cut. We want to give him a cake tomorrow..."

"This cake is for Arnold Palmer?" the manager said, cutting Jacobsen off.

"Yes."

"I can have it for you tonight."

Players who were there still remember that afternoon when the cake was presented to Palmer.

"He cut every piece for every player," Davis Love III said. "He thanked every guy individually. It really was something to see."

A few years later, Palmer still remembered that day fondly. "It meant a lot to me, not just because Peter and the others went to the trouble to do it, but because I thought it said something," Palmer said. "It said they still thought of me as one of them, that I still had a place in their world and that they cared about what I thought and what I said.

"I never wanted to be on any kind of pedestal. I never thought of myself that way. I just wanted to play good golf and treat people well. If I did that, then I always believed people would return the favor. They've done that—in spades."

U.S. Open, Oakmont Country Club,
Oakmont, PA, June 1973

The year 1960 was when Palmer went from

being a very good golfer to a legendary figure in all of sports. He had failed to win a major in 1959 and, having turned thirty in September of that year, very much wanted to add to his victory at the Masters.

Once again, the major roadblock on the final Sunday at Augusta was Ken Venturi. Palmer trailed him by a shot standing on the 17th tee with Venturi already safely in the clubhouse. The birdie holes on the back nine at Augusta were the two par 5s—13 and 15—both designed to be reachable in two as long as a player is willing to risk getting his ball wet along the way. The final two holes were best played—as they are today—with par in mind.

But Palmer needed at least one birdie to tie Venturi and force an eighteen-hole play-off as he stood on the 17th tee. Undaunted, he rolled in a long birdie putt at the 17th and then hit his approach shot at 18 to five feet. When that birdie putt went into the hole, Palmer had pulled off one of the more remarkable comebacks in Masters history to beat Venturi again and win his second green jacket.

U.S. Open, Olympic Club,
San Francisco, CA, June 1966

The *way* Palmer won his second major title boosted his celebrity as much as the simple fact that he had won it. The back-to-back birdies, the little jig he did on the 18th green after making his putt—a moment still shown every spring as part of the pre-game Masters television broadcast—and the way he carried himself quickly made Palmer an iconic figure. He wasn't just on the cover of *Sports Illustrated*; he was on the cover of *Time* and *Newsweek*. Endorsement deals came at him left and right. The day after he won the Masters, President Eisenhower flew to Augusta to play golf with him. Eisenhower was the first of six presidents Palmer played golf with. No doubt each of the six would say the privilege was theirs. If anyone could cross political party lines, it was Arnold Palmer.

Of course, there was still more to do. He hadn't yet won a U.S. Open. The U.S. Open, at Cherry Hills, didn't begin very well for him that year. Attempting to drive the green at the short 351-yard par-4 1st hole, Palmer pushed the shot right into a creek bed and began the championship with a double bogey 6. After three rounds he was tied for fifteenth place, seven shots behind leader Mike Souchak.

At lunchtime that day, The Legend of Arnold Palmer was locked into golfing lore forever. To say that was a different time is a vast understatement. Back then the Open was played over three days with a thirty-six-hole finish on Saturday. That meant the players finished their morning rounds, grabbed a quick lunch in the clubhouse, and then headed back out for eighteen more holes in the

FOLLOWING: U.S. Open, Oakmont Country Club, Oakmont, PA, June 1973

With Dwight Eisenhower, PGA Championship, Laurel Valley Golf Club, Ligonier, PA, July 1965

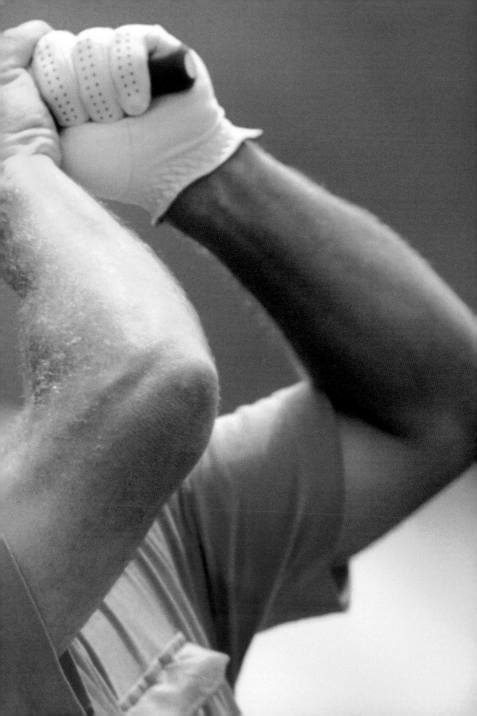

afternoon. It was also a time when players—especially Palmer—had close relationships with reporters. There were no interview rooms, no cameras recording players getting out of their cars, no coterie of security guards around the stars everywhere they went.

And so it was that Palmer, the world's No. 1 golfer, sat in the clubhouse and had lunch with two reporters: Bob Drum, then of the *Pittsburgh Press*, and Dan Jenkins, then of the *Fort Worth News*. He considered both men friends. Which is why it wasn't all that surprising that he would confide to them that he was planning to drive the 1st green—just as he had tried unsuccessfully to do on Thursday.

"If I can drive the first green and shoot 65, I can win," Palmer told Drum and Jenkins.

Both men laughed and pointed out that (a) he probably couldn't drive the green, and (b) he was trailing fourteen players, among them forty-seven-year-old Ben Hogan and twenty-year-old amateur Jack Nicklaus.

"If I shoot 65, that will give me 280," Palmer said. "Doesn't 280 always win the Open?"

"Yeah," Jenkins answered. "When Hogan shoots it."

Palmer stalked off and showed up on the 1st tee soon after that with his driver in his hands. He crushed his tee shot, bouncing it onto the green, the ball skidding to a stop about twenty feet from the cup. Palmer was so pumped up he blew his putt for an eagle about four feet past the hole. But he made the putt coming back and went from there.

U.S. Open, Congressional Country
Club, Bethesda, MD, June 1964

To this day, that afternoon is considered one of the most historic in golf. The young Nicklaus was paired with the old Hogan and actually held the lead briefly on the back nine. Hogan, blunt as always, said afterward, "I just played with a kid who would have won the Open going away if he had known what he was doing."

Nicklaus didn't win, though, and neither did Hogan. Palmer did—shooting 65 for 280 after driving the 1st green. Talk about calling your shot! And, unlike with Babe Ruth, there is no doubt that the story is true, since there were two reporters who heard what Palmer said he was going to do before he went out and did it.

That Open put Palmer halfway to a grand slam. Except in those days no one really talked about a grand slam. Very few American players even went to the British Open in those days. It was a long, difficult trip whether one opted for a bumpy airplane flight or a crossing in an ocean liner, which took five to seven days. The prize money was a fraction of what American players had grown accustomed to, and being awarded the Claret Jug, while important, wasn't nearly as prestigious as winning the Masters or the U.S. Open.

Palmer changed all that. He decided to go after he won at Cherry Hills. Palmer didn't mind flying; he *loved* flying. He had bought his first airplane to celebrate his second win at the Masters. Years later, talking about how golf had changed, he remembered buying that first plane. "I bought it after I'd won the Masters twice," he said. "Now, if a guy wins anywhere *once*, he goes out and buys a plane."

Baltusrol Golf Club, Springfield, NJ,
August 1964

Palmer wanted to make the trip in 1960 because the Open was being held at the Old Course at St. Andrews, the oldest golf course in the world. So he flew over and, just as Hogan did in 1953, had to play thirty-six holes of qualifying in order to get into the tournament even though he had just won back-to-back majors. Back then everyone, even the defending champion, had to play qualifying. Palmer played well in the championship, especially for someone playing links golf in major championship conditions for the first time, but finished second—one shot behind Kel Nagle.

The closest Palmer had come to playing links golf prior to St. Andrews was in Bing Crosby's tournament at Pebble Beach. But a California links is entirely different from a Scottish links. The only time Palmer had come close to playing in Scotland had been in 1955—when he had planned to play in the British Amateur. But after winning the U.S. Amateur, he turned pro at the end of 1954 and thus was making his first trip to Scotland for the 1960 Open Championship.

As always, the importance of Palmer's presence went well beyond the result of the game. Because Palmer had talked about wanting to win all four majors—the PGA Championship had become a stroke play event two years earlier and had finally been accepted by all in golf as a major—the term *grand slam* was used for the first time to describe the Masters, the U.S. Open, the British Open, and the PGA. Now those four are known as the modern-day slam, so that when people say no one has ever won a calendar-year slam, no one gets confused and asks, "What about Bobby Jones in 1930?"

FOLLOWING: U.S. Open, Baltusrol Golf Club, Springfield, NJ, June 1967

Carling World Open, Oakland Hills Country Club, Bloomfield Hills, MI, August 1964

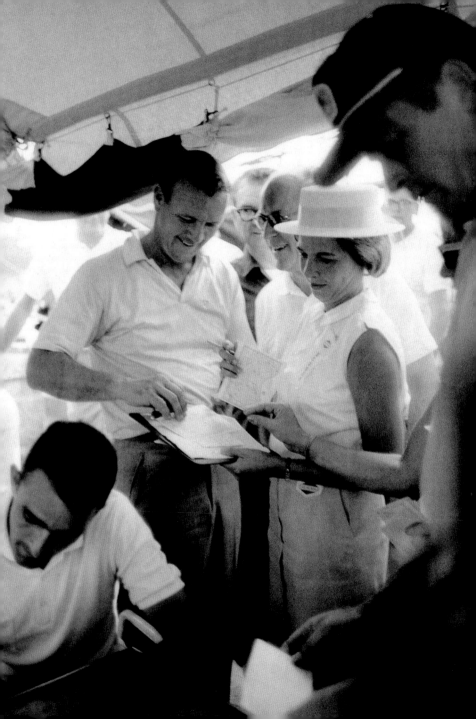

In a very real sense, Palmer created the modern slam by traveling to play in the British Open in 1960 after winning the Masters and the U.S Open. Just winning the first *two* majors in a given year is a remarkable feat. Only two other players have matched what Palmer did in 1960: Jack Nicklaus, in 1972, and Tiger Woods, in 2002. Hogan remains the only man to win the Masters, the U.S. Open, and the British Open in the same year, in 1953.

Just as important, by going to St. Andrews, Palmer also made the British Open relevant again. Most American players took their cue at that point from Arnie. So if he was willing to travel to play the British Open—regardless of the prize money—that meant it was worth the trip.

Palmer went back to the British Open a total of twenty-three times. He won it twice, in 1961 at the Royal Birkdale Golf Club and in 1962 at the Royal Troon Golf Club—beating Nagle at Troon by six shots in one of his most dominating performances. By then he was probably as popular in the British Isles as he was in the United States, and that is saying quite a lot. No one appreciates golf more than those who grow up in Great Britain—*especially* the Scots. Just as they would do later with Jack Nicklaus and Tom Watson, they made Palmer an adopted son.

Watson, who won the British Open five times and almost won it a sixth time, in 2009, at the age of fifty-nine, has an explanation for why the Scots have taken to great American players the way they have through the years. "Golf in Scotland is a lot like baseball is in the U.S.," Watson said. "Almost everyone grows up with the game.

U.S. Open, Olympic Club, San
Francisco, CA, June 1966

Regardless of how well they play the game, all Scots *understand* the game. They don't go out to golf tournaments because they want to go sit in a corporate tent or want to tell their buddies they were there. They go to watch *golf*—that's why it doesn't matter what the weather is, you see the Scots out playing and, when there's a tournament going on, watching.

"When Arnold went over there in 1960, they understood what it meant to their Open Championship. They appreciated it. They understood his magnetism and his greatness, and that's why they were thrilled when he won over there twice in a row. I honestly think if Arnold had ever gone head-to-head with one of their own for an Open Championship, loyal as they are to their own, it would have been very hard for them to pull against Arnold."

The phrase *Arnie's Army* had first appeared in the *Augusta Chronicle* during the 1958 Masters to describe a group of soldiers from Fort Bragg who had come to Augusta to cheer on Palmer. That army had grown—first at Augusta, then around the United States, before it crossed the Atlantic to Great Britain. Eventually it would spread around the world.

If Palmer had beaten Nagle in 1960, he might very well have won the modern grand slam. He finished tied for seventh that year at the PGA Championship, but who knows how inspired he might have been had a grand slam still been possible.

Palmer was also primarily responsible for the Royal and Ancient Golf Club of St. Andrews, which runs the British Open, finally relenting on its rule that all players had to qualify each year

U.S. Open, Olympic Club, San Francisco, CA, June 1966

FOLLOWING: U.S. Open, Baltusrol Country Club, Springfield, NJ, June 1967

for the event. After his victory at Troon, Palmer let it be known that if he had to go through qualifying *again* in order to get into the tournament in 1963, he might consider skipping the British Open so he could be better rested to play the PGA—which he had not yet won—three weeks later. Suddenly, the R&A became more willing to reconsider its rules on qualifying.

Of course, Palmer never did win a PGA—the one and only true hole on his golf résumé. He finished tied for second three times, including in 1964, when he and Jack Nicklaus finished three shots behind Bobby Nichols; in 1968, when he and Bob Charles finished a shot behind Julius Boros; and in 1970, when Dave Stockton shot 279 at Southern Hills and Palmer and Bob Murphy shot 281. Close, but no Wanamaker Trophy. Unlike a lot of athletes who rationalize their failures, Palmer has always been honest about the disappointment of not winning a PGA.

"When I was young, the Amateur was certainly a bigger deal than the PGA," he said. "In some ways, it was as big as any major. But that changed, especially after the PGA became a stroke play event and it was played on some great golf courses. The year I won the Masters and the British, it was played at Firestone—that's a great golf course. I had a lot of wins that I'm very proud to have. But I would have liked to have had one PGA."

Palmer ended up winning the Masters four times. He won it a third time in 1962, when he again had a chance to win a grand slam. He was very much at the peak of his powers and his popularity when that year began. He had played extremely well in

U.S. Open, Oakmont Country Club,
Oakmont, PA, June 1973

1961—winning six tournaments, including the British Open. He also finished tied for second at the Masters and fifth at the PGA. His only non–top ten finish in a major had come at the U.S. Open, where he had tied for fourteenth place.

At the beginning of 1962, he picked up right where he had left off—winning the Palm Springs Golf Classic (now the Bob Hope Desert Classic) and the Phoenix Open Invitational. He won his third Masters by beating Gary Player and his pal Dow Finsterwald in a play-off. That sent him to Oakmont Country Club for the U.S. Open on a roll that had seen him win four of nine majors dating to

Baltusrol Golf Club, Springfield, NJ,
August 1964

the start of 1960 while finishing second on two other occasions. He had finished out of the top ten once—the tie for fourteenth at the 1961 U.S. Open. Those are the kinds of numbers associated these days with Tiger Woods.

In the years since that famous U.S. Open in 1962, Palmer has often said that his play-off loss there to Jack Nicklaus was one of the great disappointments of his career. Oakmont was like a home away from home for Palmer, located about forty miles from Latrobe, just outside Pittsburgh. Arnie's Army seemed to have recruited the navy, the marines, and the air force to back it up that

ABOVE: PGA Championship, Laurel Valley Golf Club, Ligonier, PA, July 1965

FOLLOWING: Bing Crosby National Pro-Am, Pebble Beach Golf Links, Pebble Beach, CA, January 1966

weekend. Some who were there think that the screaming Palmer fans helped focus Nicklaus, who was as steely-eyed at twenty-two as he would be throughout his brilliant career.

Nicklaus took a three-shot lead early in the eighteen-hole play-off, which was on Father's Day Sunday. (It wasn't until 1965 that the USGA abandoned the thirty-six-hole Saturday finish in favor of playing four eighteen-hole rounds from Thursday to Sunday.) Palmer rallied to close the gap to one, before Nicklaus rebuilt his lead late and won by three shots.

In many ways, the ending was typical of Palmer: after he had missed a par putt on the 18th hole that meant Nicklaus only had to tap in to win by three, he graciously picked up Nicklaus's mark and went to shake hands and congratulate him. Except in stroke play there are no conceded putts. Every player has to putt out on every hole, regardless of the length of the putt or the margin one player has over another on the 18th hole. In the fog of his disappointment, Palmer simply forgot. USGA officials rushed onto the green to find the spot where Nicklaus's mark had been so he could putt out—which he finally did.

The victory marked a beginning for Nicklaus and—some thought—an ending for Palmer. As it turned out, though, Palmer had other ideas. He knew Nicklaus was going to be a great player—he'd known it since Nicklaus finished second at Cherry Hills—but that didn't mean he was ready for a rocking chair at the age of thirty-two.

One month after the disappointment of Oakmont, Palmer

U.S. Open, Baltusrol Golf Club, Springfield, NJ, June 1967

FOLLOWING: U.S. Open, Olympic Club, San Francisco, CA, June 1966

won his second straight British Open. Nicklaus was nowhere to be found on Sunday, finishing twenty-nine shots behind Palmer. No one else in the field came within six shots of him as he breezed to his fifth major title. The all-time record for professional major titles was Walter Hagen's eleven. Palmer was almost halfway there and appeared to have a lot of great golf ahead of him. Even though many had been properly awed by Nicklaus's performance at Oakmont, Palmer had been one missed putt from winning that championship and the year's first three majors.

In fact, that year was arguably his best on tour—two wins in majors and eight victories total. A year later he was almost as good, winning seven tournaments in all. For some reason, Palmer never fared as well in odd-numbered years in the events that mattered most as he did in even-numbered years. His only major win in an odd-numbered year came in the 1961 British Open. In 1963, he came achingly close again at the U.S. Open, this time losing, with Jacky Cupit, in a three-man play-off to Julius Boros.

It is a mark of just how good Palmer was during that period that a year in which he won seven tournaments might be considered a disappointment. Palmer's fifteen wins in '62 and '63 rank as one of the most dominating periods any golfer has ever had. He began 1964 by casting aside any notion of going winless in the majors for another year. He won the Masters by six shots—the first win at Augusta that allowed him to walk up the 18th fairway with victory at hand, soaking up the cheers without having to worry about losing focus with the tournament still in doubt.

U.S. Open, Oakmont Country Club,
Oakmont, PA, June 1973

"That was one of the best feelings I've ever had in golf," he said, years later. "The other times I won at Augusta, or lost at the very end, I had to try to keep my concentration until the last putt was in the hole. The one time I did look around was when I made the mistake of going over to the ropes in '61, and it ended up costing me."

Tom Kite, the 1992 U.S. Open champion, once made the point that a golfer never knows when he's won his last tournament, because at the moment he wins it he's playing so well that he assumes he will keep winning forever. Certainly no one, least of all Palmer, could have guessed that his fourth win at Augusta would be his last victory in a major championship. He was not yet thirty-five years old and was still at the top of his game and his sport.

But when defending champion Jack Nicklaus slipped the green jacket onto his shoulders in April 1964, it was the last ceremony at a major where he got to give a victory speech. It wasn't as if he fell off the golf map; quite the opposite. By then, Nicklaus and Gary Player had both become multiple-major champions too and, since Palmer had arranged for each of them to be represented by Mark McCormack and the International Management Group, the three stars were marketed together as The Big Three.

They had their own TV show, *Big Three Golf*, and were often matched in exhibitions for big money. They were the perfect foils for one another: Palmer was the star, the charming, handsome guy whom everyone rooted for on good days or bad. Nicklaus was

U.S. Open, Olympic Club, San
Francisco, CA, June 1966

the talent, the guy who hit shots to the moon, made every clutch putt, and gave Arnie's Army someone to root against. And Player was the outsider, the little guy from South Africa who didn't have Palmer's charisma or Nicklaus's talent but buzzed around like the Energizer Bunny finding ways to compete and win and captivate the crowd with his boundless enthusiasm.

In his book *Arnie & Jack: Palmer, Nicklaus, and Golf's Greatest Rivalry,* author Ian O'Connor asks Palmer why he was willing to bolster the career of a player who was clearly destined to be his greatest rival, by setting Nicklaus up with McCormack. "I just liked him," Palmer answered. "And I knew he was going to be good for golf."

Palmer was smart enough to know that what was good for golf was good for him. But he also had—and has—such a deep affection for the sport that he was always willing to help young players, even a young player who would end up denying him a number of major championships.

Nicklaus and Player would eventually leave McCormack to start their own companies. They would continue to compete with Palmer on the golf course and in the golf course design business, which all three became heavily involved in as they grew older. But the notion of The Big Three never went away. It has never again been repeated in golf or in any other sport with the kind of success that Palmer, Nicklaus, and Player had in their heyday.

And while Palmer's period as the No. 1 player ended earlier than he would have liked, that did nothing to diminish his popu-

PGA Championship, Laurel Valley
Golf Club, Ligonier, PA, July 1965

larity or his marketability. Well into his seventies, when he was a part-time player on the Champions Tour, Palmer was still the No. 1 moneymaker among professional athletes each year. He played for as long as he did in part because he loved being out there, but also because he knew people still wanted to see him play—even if he often found his own failings painful.

After his victory at the Masters in 1964, he was still a very competitive player for another ten years. In fact, he won eighteen more times on tour and had several opportunities to add to his list of major titles. The most famous—or infamous—of those chances came at the U.S. Open at the Olympic Club in 1966, when he appeared to be poised for a runaway, record-setting victory. With nine holes to play, Palmer led Billy Casper by seven shots and thought he had a good chance to break Ben Hogan's all-time U.S. Open scoring record of 276. All he had to do was shoot a two-over-par 37 on the back nine.

Palmer was so comfortably in the lead that he actually spent time on the 10th fairway counseling Casper to hang in there, so he could hold on to second place. Casper was a major champion himself—he'd won the U.S. Open in 1959—so it wasn't as if he was some kid who needed a pep talk. But Palmer, as competitive as he was, always wanted to help the other guy out when he could. Before he knew it, Casper had made a couple of putts and Palmer had lost focus and made a couple of mistakes, and his lead had disappeared. When Palmer missed a birdie putt on 18, the two men finished tied at 278. Stunned by what had happened, Palmer lost

U.S. Open, Oakmont Country Club,
Oakmont, PA, June 1973

the play-off—the third time in five years he lost the U.S. Open in a play-off—by three strokes the next day.

It was, without question, the most stunning defeat of his career. And even though he would be in the hunt at majors as late as the 1973 U.S. Open, when he was among the leaders whom Johnny Miller caught with his amazing Sunday 63 at Oakmont (Palmer finished tied for fourth), he never came that close to winning a major championship again.

Palmer did manage to win again before the end of 1966—at Houston—and he won four times in 1967 but again finished second in the U.S. Open, this time beaten by Nicklaus's brilliant Sunday 65 at Baltusrol Golf Club. In a last twist of the knife, Nicklaus broke Hogan's U. S. Open scoring record.

In 1994, after he had returned to Oakmont to play in his final U.S. Open, Palmer was completely overwhelmed by the reaction of his fans throughout his final round. On a searingly hot, humid day, thousands followed him for eighteen holes, wanting to witness his last round in an Open. When the round ended, with Palmer shooting 81, he shook his head in disbelief at the way he had been treated.

"Any other sport, I would have been booed for the way I played today," he said. "To get that kind of reaction, to have people cheer for me the way they did . . ." His voice trailed off as he began to break down. "I played some good golf through the years. I won a few times. But to have people do that..."

He stopped. He was crying. Of course, Palmer had become to golf fans—and so many others—far more than someone who

U.S. Open, Baltusrol Golf Club,
Springfield, NJ, June 1967

played some good golf and won a few times. Aside from the fact that winning sixty-two times on the PGA Tour, seven professional majors, and a U.S. Amateur title goes well beyond "winning a few times," his accomplishments and his importance to his sport simply can't be measured in numbers.

What Palmer did, long after he won that last major in 1964, was touch people. He did it every day, and he did it—seemingly—without effort. If Nicklaus and Woods were born to play golf, Palmer was born to win people's hearts. It came as naturally to him as making clutch putts came to Nicklaus and Woods. He never had to think about doing it; he just did it.

Palmer continued to be a very good player right through 1973—the year he turned forty-four. He won at least once on tour every year from 1955—his rookie year—through 1971. That streak of seventeen straight years with at least one win has been matched by only one other player—Nicklaus. Palmer failed to win in 1972 for the first time in his professional career but began the next year with an emotional win—beating Nicklaus and Johnny Miller down the stretch—at one of his favorite events, the Bob Hope Desert Classic. It was the fifth time he had won in the desert, and it turned out to be his last victory on tour.

He had other chances to win, notably at the 1975 Hawaiian Open, where he finished two shots behind a tour journeyman named Gary Groh—who had never won before on tour and never won again. Bob Green, the longtime golf writer for the Associated Press, covered that tournament. Like those of most AP writers,

PGA Championship, Laurel Valley
Golf Club, Ligonier, PA, July 1965

Green's stories were usually very straight and to the point. One would have expected from Green something along the lines of, "Gary Groh fired a final round 69 on Sunday to win the Hawaiian Open by one shot over Hale Irwin and Al Geiberger and two shots over Arnold Palmer."

That wasn't Green's lede. Instead, he wrote simply, "Arnie lost again."

"That was the story," Green said, when the subject of that first paragraph came up. "No offense to Gary Groh, but what most people reading that story wanted to know was, how did Arnie do? You write for your readers. The readers cared about Arnold Palmer more than Gary Groh."

One person who agreed with Green's decision was Gary Groh. "I made forty thousand dollars for winning that day," he said. "My guess is first-place money wouldn't have been half of that if not for Arnold Palmer. Every single one of us playing golf for a living owes part of that living to Arnold. He made our game what it is today. If I'd have been writing that story, I would have done the exact same thing."

Remember that Palmer was forty-five years old at the time, well past his prime, and had won once—the victory at the '73 Hope—in four years. Even so, everyone agreed that Palmer coming close and not winning was still a bigger story than anyone else winning.

That may be what made Palmer different from so many athletes. When great athletes begin to fade, most of us avert our eyes.

British Open, St. Andrews, Scotland,
July 1978

No one wants to remember Willie Mays stumbling around in center field for the Mets in the 1973 World Series, or Johnny Unitas in a San Diego Chargers uniform, or Michael Jordan as a Washington Wizard.

Some might say golf is different, because the great ones can still go out and make a dramatic birdie—the way Nicklaus did on the 18th hole of his final round at the British Open in 2005—but even then, age has clearly dulled that which made those golfers brilliant. No one went kicking and screaming into the twilight with more fury than Nicklaus. In 2001, when the Augusta green jackets paired Nicklaus, Palmer, and Player in a nostalgic threesome on the first two days of the tournament, Nicklaus was furious.

"I am *not* a ceremonial golfer," Nicklaus said. "I'm just crazy enough to think I can still win."

Of course, he couldn't. He missed the cut and left still angry that he had been paired with his two old pals and business partners.

Palmer didn't like it when he couldn't play the way he once did either. Even as he got older, he continued to work on his game, pounding balls on the practice tee with as much intensity as when he was a teenager at Latrobe Country Club. He continued to fiddle constantly with clubs, looking for the secret that would unlock his skills one more time.

Deep down, though, he understood that he was no longer the guy who had driven that 1st green at Cherry Hills in 1960 or won the back-to-back British Opens or the four Masters in seven years. But he *was* still Arnold Palmer, and he knew people loved to

U.S. Open, Olympic Club, San Francisco, CA, June 1966

see him walking the fairways, still making the occasional birdie, still piecing together a solid round every now and then—notably the two days at Bay Hill in 1991 when he made the cut at the age of sixty-one.

Where Nicklaus only grudgingly played on the Senior PGA Tour, Palmer embraced it, not only because it was a place where he could compete, but also because he knew—as he always knew—that it benefited his sport and the players he had grown up with. He was thrilled to have the chance to compete again, to once more feel the thrill of the hunt on Sunday and the adrenaline rush that comes with winning.

But playing on the Senior Tour was more than that for Palmer. It gave him a chance to hear fans cheer, to be a part of the Army again, when he was seriously competing. Plus, he knew it wasn't a coincidence that the PGA Tour had decided to launch a tour for the over-fifty set soon after he turned fifty. Without Palmer, there wouldn't have been a Senior Tour. It was Dave Marr who called that tour "life's ultimate mulligan." It was Palmer who made that mulligan possible for every player who has ever teed it up on what is now called the Champions Tour.

As he had always done, Palmer embraced his role as the star of the new tour. He still wanted to play occasionally with the kids on the regular tour, and he had lots of work to do away from the course. But he found time to play the Senior Tour because he understood how important he was to its success. From 1983 through 2000, he played at least twelve times every year but one—

PGA Championship, Laurel Valley
Golf Club, Ligonier, PA, July 1965

when he played ten times—and frequently played as many as seventeen or eighteen times per year. In fact, from 1989 to 1993, he played at least seventeen times each year. It is probably not a coincidence that during those years, the Senior Tour was at the height of its popularity.

The most Senior Tour events Jack Nicklaus ever played in a year was nine—and that was in 2003, when he was winding down and making final appearances at a number of places. More typically he played between five and seven events each year—most of them the senior majors. Nicklaus could never wrap his head around the idea that a fifty-four-hole tournament with no cut was a real competition.

Palmer had no such problem. For one thing, he understood that the Senior Tour was as much about entertainment as it was about competition. He knew that the fans were thrilled to see him out on the golf course whether it was at Augusta or at the Outback Steakhouse Pro-Am in Lutz, Florida. He still wanted to play well— and he did, winning ten times on the Senior Tour, including five majors. But he also understood, especially in the later years, that his presence in a tournament lent a luster to it that had absolutely nothing to do with how he scored.

That said, his victory at the second U.S. Senior Open was critical because it put senior golf on the map in a way no other player could. All of a sudden, television came running, wanting to air senior tournaments because they would get Arnold Palmer on TV again, playing in serious competition. Ask anyone who

U.S. Open, Olympic Club, San Francisco, CA, June 1966

FOLLOWING: U.S. Open, Congressional Country Club, Bethesda, MD, June 1964

has ever played the Senior Tour how important Palmer's role was at the beginning—and for years after that—and they will gladly tell you.

"There's not a lot of magic in over-fifty golf," said Jeff Sluman, who has played the Champions Tour for the past four years. "It's a bunch of guys who can still play but can't quite play at the highest level trying to grind out a pretty good living. Arnold brought the magic. He was the guy people came to see, especially at the start. You look at all the other great players who have come out here and played, and they're terrific. But none of them can bring the attention or the flair or the wonder of it all the way Arnold did. It's no knock on anyone else to say this: there's only one Arnold Palmer.

"Jack was amazing, Tiger is unbelievable. But Arnold was unique. I'm not sure I ever heard of anyone rooting *against* Arnold Palmer."

Palmer very much enjoyed his second golfing life on the Senior Tour. He enjoyed the camaraderie in the locker room with players who were close to him in age, and he liked winning again. He didn't win again on the regular tour after the victory at the Hope in 1973, so when he won the Senior PGA Championship in 1980 (he was able to play that year because the PGA of America had always considered fifty the age when one became a senior player, even before the USGA and PGA Tour changed their age rules for Palmer), it was his first victory in a "real" tournament in seven years. He would win nine times over the next six years

PGA Championship, PGA National
Golf Club, Palm Beach Gardens, FL,
February 1971

and be in contention on many other occasions. Put simply, having that feeling again was fun.

"I like to play good golf," he said in the mid-1990s, when he was well into his sixties and still playing close to a full schedule on the Senior Tour. "I know I'm older now and I can't hit it as far as I once did, but I still believe I have some good golf left in me. Playing bad golf isn't fun. I love being out there, I love the interaction with the fans and with the other players, but I don't enjoy it if I play badly. That's why I still practice as much as I do, and that's why I get frustrated when I'm not playing well.

"When the Senior Tour started, I was one of the young guys out there, and I played well. It was different than when I started on tour in my twenties, but it was fun again. The last few years on the regular tour weren't that much fun, because even though I told myself I was going out there to try and win the tournament whenever I played, I knew realistically that time had passed me by. When I went out on the Senior Tour, the chance to win became real again. That was a good feeling."

Throughout those years, Palmer continued to play the Masters every spring. Although Nicklaus won more Masters (six to Palmer's four) and became a beloved figure with the crowds at Augusta, no one inspired adoration the way Palmer did. Often when Palmer was on the golf course during his final years as a player, it felt as if fifty thousand people were watching him and five hundred were watching the rest of the field. Every single time he walked up the hill to the 18th green—whether during a

PGA Championship, Laurel Valley
Golf Club, Ligonier, PA, July 1965

practice round or a tournament round—the ovation went on and on...and on.

Playing a practice round with Palmer at the Masters became something other pros aspired to. In 1996, when Paul Goydos won for the first time on tour, at Bay Hill, the first question he asked when Palmer presented him with the trophy was, "Mr. Palmer, will you play a practice round with me at Augusta?"

By winning at Bay Hill, Goydos had qualified for his first Masters. Palmer, being Palmer, looked at him and said, "Only if you shave that thing you've got growing around your mouth."

Goydos had grown a goatee that week for reasons he has never fully explained. Not only did he shave it so that he could play that practice round with Palmer, but he asked the artist who draws the portraits of past champions that hang in the clubhouse at Bay Hill to remove the goatee from his rendering. "I didn't want Mr. Palmer walking by it and thinking I needed to shave," he said.

Palmer and Nicklaus are the only past Masters champions who have been invited to become members of the club. All champions become honorary members, but only Palmer and Nicklaus have been asked to become full members.

Palmer actually played not one but two farewell rounds at Augusta National. The first one came in 2002, in the midst of a controversy created when the club chairman at the time, Hootie Johnson, sent a letter to some—but not all—past champions suggesting that they come to Augusta as invited guests that year but *not* play in the golf tournament.

Bing Crosby National Pro-Am,
Pebble Beach Golf Links, Pebble
Beach, CA, January 1966

PAR 4
YARDS 285

Masters tradition had always dictated that past champions were eligible to play in the tournament for life. Other major championships put limits on how long their champions could continue to play: ten years at the U.S. Open; until the age of sixty at the British Open; until sixty-five at the PGA Championship. The Masters had never done that until Doug Ford, the 1957 champion, continued to play year after year, long after he was able to play the golf course reasonably well. Through 2001, Ford had played in a then-record forty-nine Masters Tournaments. But he had missed the cut or withdrawn for thirty consecutive years and had withdrawn

U.S. Open, Olympic Club, San
Francisco, CA, June 1966

without finishing thirty-six holes for four straight years.

The feeling among some—including Johnson—was that Ford had taken the lifelong exemption too far, not knowing when to bow out gracefully. Not wanting to single Ford out, Johnson wrote letters to several past champions who were over seventy, suggesting they come and enjoy the week in 2002 and leave it at that. Palmer was seventy-two at the time, but there was no way that Johnson would write *him* a letter asking him not to play.

Even so, Palmer was upset about how the other champions had been treated. In fact, he and Nicklaus wrote to Johnson, suggest-

ABOVE: PGA Championship, PGA National Golf Club, Palm Beach Gardens, FL, February 1971

FOLLOWING: U.S. Open, Oak Hill Country Club, Rochester, NY, June 1968

ing he had made a mistake and should reconsider. When Johnson didn't, Palmer announced that 2002 would be his last Masters Tournament. At a pretournament press conference, with Johnson sitting next to him, Palmer was asked why he had decided to make this his last Masters.

Palmer smiled, and then he winked and said, "I don't want to get one of those letters."

Only Palmer could deliver a zinger like that, one that everyone in the room knew he meant, without somehow offending the zingee. Johnson laughed as hard as anyone. Palmer ended up finishing his last round on Saturday morning because of a rain delay, and half the players in the locker room came pouring out of the clubhouse to watch him walk up 18 for the final time. The applause seemed to roll down off the giant loblolly pine trees in waves as Palmer smiled and bowed and tried to thank every single person packed around the green. It was a remarkable good-bye.

Except it wasn't good-bye. After that year's Masters, Johnson reconsidered his position. All the past champions were sent letters telling them they were welcome to play in the tournament—or, as they say at Augusta, the "toonamint"—for as many years as they wanted to play. He made a special plea to Palmer to come back and play at least one more time. Hootie Johnson did not want to go down in history as the man who drove Arnold Palmer away from the fairways of Augusta.

And so Palmer came back to play in 2003 and 2004 and said farewell to Augusta *again*. The 2004 Masters was the fiftieth

PGA Championship, PGA National
Golf Club, Palm Beach Gardens,
FL, February 1971

straight year he played in the tournament. Quite a feat for someone of whom Ben Hogan once said, "How the hell did that guy get
in the Masters?" Palmer not only got in, he won it four times and
stuck around to play for fifty straight years.

"The amazing thing was that it was as if 2002 never happened,"
said David Duval, one of the many players who found his way to
the back of the 18th green on another rainy Saturday morning. "I
remember we all just stood there looking at each other when he
walked on the green, not saying anything because we were all too
choked up to talk. The hair still goes up on the back of my spine
when I think about what that looked like and sounded like that
morning."

There have been lots of farewells for Palmer, and none of
them has ever been easy. Each has been emotional in a different
way, but all have been difficult, because the adulation genuinely
means something to him. He has, for the most part, kept his composure as he's made that final walk up 18, but it hasn't been easy.

In 1995, he played in his last British Open, opting—as Nicklaus would do ten years later—to say good-bye to golf's oldest
championship at its oldest course, St. Andrews. As they would
years later at Augusta, players packed the back of the 18th green
as Palmer's group came up the fairway on Friday afternoon. Nick
Faldo, a three-time British Open champion, brought a camera—
there were no cell phone cameras in those days—to record the
event. Palmer, who always understood the magnitude of a moment,
stopped on the Swilcan Bridge after walking off the 18th tee to

With Dwight Eisenhower, PGA
Championship, Laurel Valley Golf
Club, Ligonier, PA, July 1965

wave in all directions, to give the photographers plenty of time to take their photos, to give his playing partners and their caddies a chance to take a picture with him. Then they all peeled away and left him alone on the bridge—surrounded by thousands of people who all thought of themselves as his friends.

As luck would have it, Billy Andrade was on the 1st tee preparing to start his round as Palmer walked to the 18th green. Like a lot of golfers on tour, Andrade attended Wake Forest on an Arnold Palmer Scholarship. As soon as he was introduced and hit his tee shot off No. 1, Andrade rushed over to the adjacent 18th green to shake the great man's hand.

"That was one of my most memorable moments in golf," Andrade said later. "To be teeing off at that moment, when my all-time hero was walking up the 18th to that ovation, was just unreal. I've always thought how lucky I was that day. If I'd been one pairing earlier I would have missed it, because I'd have been down on the green. I'd have seen it from a distance. When I shook Arnold's hand, he just looked at me and said, 'Make me proud out there today.' I couldn't think of a thing to say, and if I had, I doubt it would have come out of my mouth anyway. I was too choked up."

The most remarkable of the farewells was the one at Oakmont, at the 1994 U.S. Open. Prior to the start of the tournament, Palmer and Nicklaus held a joint press conference to talk about their memories of the 1962 Open at Oakmont, when Nicklaus won by three shots, and their friendship, which had grown through

PGA Championship, PGA National
Golf Club, Palm Beach Gardens,
FL, February 1971

the years. Palmer talked about the first time he had come to Oakmont with his father in the early 1940s. "I still remember they were building the [Pennsylvania] Turnpike back then," he said. "It wasn't even open yet."

Nicklaus leaned over and whispered something in Palmer's ear.

"Yes, Jack, they *did* have cars back then," Palmer answered, while the entire room broke up.

Palmer actually played a decent round of golf on Thursday of that week on a difficult course. He shot 77 to put himself within shouting distance of the cut, ramming a ten-foot par putt into the back of the hole on 18 with darkness rapidly approaching.

"I can't believe how long it took us to play out there," he said. (It took five hours and twenty minutes.) "Back in '62, even when Jack was at his absolute slowest we got around in four and a half hours in threesomes."

Palmer was always a fast player, Nicklaus always about as slow as one could possibly be. Thirty-six years after they first played a round of golf together, Palmer hadn't forgotten—and wasn't about to let Nicklaus forget.

The next day was brutally hot. The Pittsburgh area was in the midst of a record heat wave, with the heat index well over one hundred degrees every day that week. Friday was no exception. By the time Palmer and the other two members of his threesome, Rocco Mediate and John Mahaffey, made the turn, the midday heat was searing.

U.S. Open, Congressional Country
Club, Bethesda, MD, June 1964

Even so, Palmer seemed to want to greet every single person who called his name or clapped or yelled encouragement to him. He actually played well for nine holes before the heat got to him, as it did that day to a lot of players who were not almost sixty-five years old. Palmer managed to summon his strength to hit the 18th green in regulation. As he began to walk toward the green, Mediate and Mahaffey dropped behind him, as did everyone else—officials, caddies, media—walking inside the ropes.

"At that moment we were all fans," Mediate said later. "I know why I got to play with Arnold those two days; because the USGA

With Jack Nicklaus, U.S. Open, Baltusrol Country Club, Springfield, NJ, June 1967

understood it was symbolic: a kid who grew up right near Latrobe with Arnold Palmer as his hero. But heck, I could have been any kid from anywhere in the country and it still would have been the same story.

"My back was killing me that day. I could barely bend over to pick the ball up out of the cup." (Mediate was not exaggerating. He made the cut but was forced to withdraw the next day because of his back and had surgery not long after that.) "But it didn't matter. I knew I had a ringside seat for a historic moment, and I was just happy to be there."

U.S. Open, Pebble Beach Golf
Links, Pebble Beach, CA, June
1972

This was the one time that Palmer lost his composure. As he walked onto the green and looked around and flashed back to playing at Oakmont as a teenager, he thought about his father, and about his boyhood dream to be a professional golfer, to make a living playing the game and to someday win on the PGA Tour. His life had gone well beyond anything he had dreamed, and now here were thousands of people screaming for him even at the end of what he thought was a disappointing round of golf.

"It just all kicked in at once," he said. "I just realized how unbelievably lucky I had been to lead the life I've led. People have been so good to me for so many years."

Of course, people were so good to him for so many years because he was good to them.

After he had holed his final putt and had been hugged by Mediate and Mahaffey, he was taken to the media tent, a routine event for him, something he had done hundreds of times in his life. On this day, it was all too much for him. The room was packed. All over the golf course, players like Ernie Els and Colin Montgomerie and Tom Watson and Loren Roberts and John Cook were fighting for the lead in the U.S. Open. No one in the media was out watching them. They were all squeezed into the giant tent that was about one hundred yards from the 18th green.

On several occasions Palmer tried to talk. He simply couldn't do it. Briefly he talked about how fortunate he'd been, how lucky he felt, but each time, the man who so many in the room had heard wax eloquent on almost any subject for years

U.S. Open, Pebble Beach Golf Links, Pebble Beach, California, June 1972

FOLLOWING: British Open, St. Andrews, Scotland, July 1978

couldn't get to the end of his sentence. Finally he said softly, "I think I better go."

No one complained. The tears had said all that needed to be said. As soon as Palmer stood up, so did everyone else in the room—applauding. It is a strict rule that reporters are not to cheer in the press box or applaud at the end of an interview. They are there to do a job, to report back to the fans, who don't have the access to the athletes that they have. If they want to cheer or applaud, they are welcome to make as much noise as they want—they just need to do it in the stands or outside the ropes and without a press credential around their neck.

On very few occasions, those rules are broken. It happened in 1980, when the U.S. hockey team beat the Soviet Union in the Lake Placid Olympics. It happened when Tom Watson tearfully talked in the press room at Augusta about his caddie and best friend Bruce Edwards on the morning that Edwards died of ALS in April 2004.

And it happened when Arnold Palmer stood up to leave the media tent at Oakmont in 1994. Everyone was on their feet, applauding. Palmer stopped at the exit to the tent and waved in appreciation as the applause went on. The standing ovation wasn't so much for the career he'd had as for the man he'd been. Almost every person in that tent had been helped at some point in his or her career by Palmer. He'd always had time—or made time—for reporters. This was their way of saying thank you, damn the rules.

Palmer has had many other farewells—the last time he played

U.S. Open, Congressional Country
Club, Bethesda, MD, June 1964

the PGA Championship, later in 1994 (ironically, the one major he never won was the last one in which he made a cut, when he finished sixty-third at Kemper Lakes Golf Club outside Chicago in 1989); the last time he played his own tournament at Bay Hill, in 2004; and his last round of competitive golf, in 2006 at a Champions Tour event.

That final day in 2006 again said a lot about Palmer: Extremely upset with his play, he formally withdrew from the tournament after four holes, because he didn't want to post a score in the 80s in his farewell to tournament golf. But because he knew that thousands of people had come to the golf course that morning only to see him play, he finished the round. Many athletes talk about playing for the fans. Arnold Palmer *lived* playing for the fans.

Which may be why the story told of how the Arnold Palmer drink—half iced tea, half lemonade—came to be named not only rings true but fits perfectly with who Arnold Palmer is.

An Arnold Palmer drink was not a marketing idea. It wasn't invented to make money or further the Palmer brand. According to Doc Giffin, who has been Palmer's publicist, right-hand man, and best friend since 1966, the story Palmer tells about how it started dates back to Palmer ordering the drink in a Palm Beach restaurant years ago.

"Arnold asked for iced tea and lemonade," Giffin says. "There was a woman sitting at the next table and when someone came to take her drink order she pointed at Arnold and said, 'I'll have an Arnold Palmer.'"

Apparently, from that moment on, the drink became known in that restaurant as an Arnold Palmer, and it spread from there, to the point where there are now people (though probably not many) who order an Arnold Palmer without knowing who Arnold Palmer is. And of course the drink is now officially marketed nationally.

It was once said of baseball Hall of Famer Reggie Jackson—by Reggie Jackson—that he was the straw that stirs the drink.

Arnold Palmer was—and is—the drink.

He is also unique in the annals of sports. The argument can be made—with little contradiction—that no athlete has been so uni-

PGA Championship, PGA National
Golf Club, Palm Beach Gardens,
FL, February 1971

versally respected and loved by fans, by the media, but perhaps most important, by his fellow players, as Arnold Palmer. He didn't always win, but he always behaved like a winner. He was gracious in both victory and defeat, no matter how galling the defeat.

Palmer turned eighty in September 2009 and remains a force in golf to this day. He still loves to play with his pals at Bay Hill and Latrobe, and players still show up every year to play in the Arnold Palmer Invitational in large part because, well, it is named for Arnold Palmer. He lost his beloved wife Winnie to cancer in 1999 after they had been married for forty-five years. Six years later, he married Kit Gawthrop, and together they help manage and raise money for the Winnie Palmer Hospital for Women and Babies.

He has won every award there is to win, including the Presidential Medal of Freedom. His numbers are staggering—the major championships, the victories on tour, the player-of-the-year awards, the Vardon Trophies (for low scoring average on tour), the money-winning titles—and on and on.

But the true measure of Arnold Palmer and his legacy goes back to Augusta, to the Masters—the major he won most often—and to his great rival Jack Nicklaus.

After Palmer retired, he was asked by Augusta National to serve as the new honorary starter for the Masters. That role has been played through the years by great Masters champions of the past. The Masters begins each year on Thursday morning with the club chairman introducing the honorary starter—or starters—at

PGA Championship, PGA National Golf Club, Palm Beach Gardens, FL, February 1971

eight in the morning. The starter hits the first tee shot of the tournament off No. 1 and the Masters is officially under way.

For many years, Gene Sarazen, Byron Nelson, and Sam Snead served together as the honorary starters. But their deaths left a void, and in 2007 Palmer was asked to fill that void. Naturally, he said yes. For three years he served alone as the honorary starter. In 2009, the club asked Jack Nicklaus to join him for the 2010 tournament—the year Nicklaus would turn seventy.

Nicklaus was reluctant. He had always said he didn't like the idea of playing ceremonial golf. Being the honorary starter—hitting one tee shot and then walking into the clubhouse—is the ultimate example of ceremonial golf. Plus, he wondered if Palmer shouldn't continue to have that stage to himself.

It was Palmer who convinced Nicklaus to do it. And so, in 2010, the two men teed it up together again at Augusta—fifty-five years after Palmer's first Masters and fifty-one years after Nicklaus's first one. Even at eight o'clock on a cool morning, spectators filled every inch of space around that 1st tee.

Nicklaus was there because Arnold Palmer told him he should be there. Everyone else was also there because of Arnold Palmer.

When Palmer made his last putt at Oakmont in 1994, Rocco Mediate wrapped his arms around him, pointed at the thousands of people surrounding them, and whispered, "All this is because of you."

Truer words have never been spoken.

New York, NY, December 1999

Acknowledgments

I would first like to thank Walter Iooss for allowing me to play a part in what is clearly his book, built around photos he has taken for more years than I can count. I would also like to thank my agent, Esther Newberg, and her assistants, Kari Stuart and Lyle Morgan, and Jennifer Levesque at Abrams Books for steering me through the project. And, of course, thanks to Arnold Palmer for the time he has given me, and so many of us in the media, through the years, and to Doc Giffin, who in almost all cases was the person responsible for arranging time with Mr. Palmer.